090l740

S0-ASM-097

ON LINE

WARS DAY BY DAY

THE CIVIL WAR

1861–1865

Ian Westwell

BROWN
BEAR
BOOKS

Published by Brown Bear Books Limited
An imprint of
The Brown Reference Group plc
68 Topstone Road
Redding
Connecticut
06896
USA
www.brownreference.com

© 2008 The Brown Reference Group plc

This hardcover edition is distributed in the United States by:
Black Rabbit Books
P.O. Box 3263
Mankato, MN 56002

ISBN: 978-1-933834-38-2

Library of Congress Cataloging-in-Publication Data

Westwell, Ian.
  The Civil War / Ian Westwell.
    p. cm. -- (Wars day by day)
  Summary: "In a time line format, describes the causes leading up to the
Civil War, events and battles during the war, and the aftermath of the war.
Includes primary source quotes"--Provided by publisher.
  Includes index.
  ISBN 978-1-933834-38-2
  1. United States--History--Civil War, 1861-1865--Juvenile literature. 2.
United States--History--Civil War, 1861-1865--Sources--Juvenile literature.
I. Title. II. Series.

E468.W475 2009
973.7--dc22

2007049999

Designer: Reg Cox
Creative Director: Jeni Child
Children's Publisher: Anne O'Daly
Editorial Director: Lindsey Lowe
Design Manager: Sarah Williams
Editor: Peter Darman

Printed and bound in the United States

Contents

Introduction 4

1850–1860 6

1861 11

1862 17

1863 23

1864 29

1865 35

1866–1877 41

Glossary 46

Further resources 47

Index 48

Introduction

The Civil War was one of the turning points in U.S. history. The bitter war was named the "War between Brothers" because Americans fought Americans. For the North the war began as a fight to preserve the Union. It ended as a crusade to free the slaves. For the South, the war was due to arguments about whether the national (federal) government should be more powerful than state governments. But how did the tensions between North and South arise?

In the northern part of America, because of the cooler climate, farms tended to grow foodstuffs. In the warmer south of the country, farmers could grow tobacco and cotton. These crops could be sold at high prices. And the more land a farmer had, the more money he could make. So in the southern part of America there was a large number of big farms. These farms were called plantations.

To make the plantations profitable required a large number of workers because the crops had to be picked by hand. The plantation owners discovered that slaves were the best workers for plantations. Slaves were owned by their masters, and could be made to work long hours in the fields. They were not seen as humans and were treated more like animals.

Slaves and slavery

By the early years of the 19th century there were millions of slaves in the South. In the North, meanwhile, there were very few slaves. Many people in the northern part of America were unhappy that humans were being used as

Hundreds of battles took place in the Civil War. This is the Battle of Cold Harbor in 1864. More than 15,000 soldiers were killed in this fight.

This map shows the side each state took in the Civil War. Four slave states remained in the Union: Missouri, Kentucky, Delaware, and Maryland. Territories were regions that were not yet states.

United States
Slave states in the United States
Territories
Confederate States

slaves. Also, the cities in the North were growing faster than those in the South. And there were more factories in the North. The growing strength of the North frightened the people of the South.

The desire to leave the Union

Those who lived in the South began to think that they would be better off if they left the United States. They did not want to be "united" with people who wanted to end slavery and also destroy their wealth. Southerners began to talk about "states' rights." This meant the right of a state to ignore the decisions of the national government to protect its own customs. One of these customs was slavery.

Many people in the North were determined to prevent states' rights. They realized it would mean the break-up of the United States. They wanted a country that was united. They were called Unionists, or supporters of the Union. In the South, people who supported states' rights wished to see their states leave the Union. This was called secession. States that wanted to break away from the Union included South Carolina, Florida, Mississippi, Georgia, Texas, and Louisiana. It made sense that they should band together, because that would make them

stronger than if each acted alone. When they did band together their group was called a Confederacy. And the people who supported the Confederacy were called Confederates.

Lincoln becomes president

The election of Abraham Lincoln as president of the United States in 1860 brought matters to a head. Lincoln was not prepared to see the break-up of the Union. But the Southern states would not be told what to do. They thought they would be better off in a country of their own. Each state voted to leave the Union.

In early 1861, the leaders of the Southern states met in Montgomery, Alabama. They set up the Confederate States of America. President Lincoln said he would not allow any state to leave the Union. Both North and South began to prepare for a civil war. That war broke out on April 12, 1861, when Confederate troops opened fire on Union troops in Fort Sumter in Charleston Harbor.

A slave pen in Alexandria, Virginia.

1852 Literature

Harriet Beecher Stowe publishes *Uncle Tom's Cabin*, a book about the cruelty of enslavement. This makes many Northerners even more determined to abolish slavery in the United States.

1853 Washington, D.C.

Senator Stephen A. Douglas of Illinois introduces a bill in Congress to organize a new territory, Nebraska. Douglas does this because he wants a new railroad to connect his hometown of Chicago with California. Southern congressmen block the bill because they want a southern route for the railroad. Douglas revises the bill to create two new territories, Kansas and Nebraska.

1850 Washington, D.C.

Congress passes a Fugitive Slave Law. It says that people who had escaped from slavery must be returned to their owners.

1851 The North

To weaken the Fugitive Slave Law, many Northern states pass "personal liberty laws." They make it difficult for plantation owners to regain escaped slaves.

1853 Canada

Mary Ann Shadd Cary, a former Southern slave, begins publishing a weekly journal, *The Provincial Freeman*, from her exile in British Canada.

Turning Points: Slavery

Slaves (seen at right) from Africa were first used as labor in the United States in the 17th century. In the South, tobacco and cotton grew on large plantations. Many people were needed to pick these crops. Large numbers of slaves were used. By 1850 there were 1,815,000 slaves in the South on cotton plantations. There were another 600,000 slaves producing other crops. Slaves were bought and sold as property. They were seen as animals, not as people.

Slave – a person who is owned by another person.

EYEWITNESS: Richard Toler, slave

"They were whipping slaves all the time, but I ran away all the time. And I just tell them—if they whipped me, I'd kill 'em, and I never did get a whipping. If I thought one was coming to me, I'd hide in the woods; then they'd send after me saying, 'Come on back, we won't whip you.' But they killed some of the slaves, whipped them to death. They never allowed us to have a book in our hand, and we couldn't have no money neither."

MAY 1854, Washington, D.C.
The Kansas-Nebraska Act is passed by Congress by a vote of 115 to 104. The bill says that settlers who move to the new territories will be allowed to decide for themselves whether Kansas and Nebraska will allow slavery.

1855 Literature
Maria Weston Chapman publishes *How Can I Help to Abolish Slavery*.

MAY 19, 1854, Washington, D.C.
Massachusetts Senator Charles Sumner is attacked on the floor of the Senate by Preston S. Brooks. Senator Sumner had made an antislavery speech attacking Senator Andrew Pickens Butler of South Carolina. Brooks was Butler's nephew.

MAY 23, 1856, Kansas
Six followers of the abolitionist John Brown kill five proslavery men at Pottawatomie Creek. Brown becomes a hate-figure for proslavers after this attck. He narrowly escapes being killed.

1857 Washington, D.C.
The Supreme Court delivers its verdict in the Dred Scott case. Dred Scott is a former black slave who lives in the North. The court decides that people of African descent can never be citizens of the United States. The case makes the situation between the North and South even worse. Tensions are mounting in the country.

Abraham Lincoln's house in Springfield, Illinois.

Abolitionist – a person who wanted to end slavery.

Slaves packing cotton in the South.

DECEMBER 2, 1859, The North

On the day of Brown's execution bells are tolled and guns fired in many places in the North. Church services and public meetings are held to remember and praise his deeds.

DECEMBER 7, 1859, New York

John Brown's body arrives in North Elba. It is laid out in the front room of his house for visiting relatives, friends, and supporters to see.

JANUARY, 1860, Virginia

Volunteer militia officers meet in Richmond, the capital of Virginia. They begin to organize the training and growth of volunteer militia units. The South is beginning to prepare for a possible war against the North.

OCTOBER 16, 1859, Virginia

John Brown leads a raid on the Federal arsenal (a store for weapons) at Harpers Ferry. His aim was to start a slave uprising that will sweep the South. He will do this by providing local slaves with weapons and ammunition.

OCTOBER 18, 1859, Virginia

Marines under U.S. Army Colonel Robert E. Lee storm the fire-engine roundhouse in which Brown and his followers have barricaded themselves. Lee's men arrest Brown with six followers. Ten of Brown's men are killed in the fighting.

DECEMBER 2, 1859, Virginia

Having been convicted of murder, John Brown is hanged at Charles Town. Despite his violent actions, many people in the North have sympathy for him. To Southerners, Brown was a murderer. But to Northerners he is a martyr. Many Southerners feel this proves that their fellow countrymen despise them. They believe it is time to go their separate ways and split from the North.

EYEWITNESS: John Brown

"I am quite cheerful in view of my approaching end, being fully persuaded that I am worth inconceivably more to hang than for any other purpose, I count it all joy. 'I have fought the good fight' and have, as I trust, finished my course."

The abolitionist John Brown to his brother after being sentenced to hang. Brown was hanged on December 2, 1859.

Martyr – someone who is prepared to die for a belief.

APRIL, 1860, North America

The Pony Express begins. This is a fast mail service from the Missouri River to the Pacific coast. Messages are carried on horseback rather than by stagecoach.

APRIL 23, 1860, South Carolina

The National Convention of the Democratic Party opens in Charleston, South Carolina. The party is divided over slavery. The party splits into two factions. The Southern Democrats are determined to have a slave code that protects slave owners. The Northern Democrats oppose a slave code.

NOVEMBER 6, 1860, Washington, D.C.

The Republican Abraham Lincoln is elected President of the United States. Lincoln will become the 16th president of the United States. He says that he will not allow the break-up of the Union.

NOVEMBER 6, 1860, Georgia

A public meeting in Johnson Square, Savannah, calls for a state secession convention to be held. The Southern states are alarmed at Lincoln becoming president. They think he will free the slaves and ruin their livelihood.

DECEMBER 17, 1860, South Carolina

The state convention meets. It votes 159 to 0 to decide that South Carolina will leave the Union. South Carolina is the first state to decide to leave the Union. President Lincoln has said he will not allow this.

The thick-walled brick building where Brown barricaded himself after the raid on Harpers Ferry.

Secession – leaving the Union.

Crowds cheering in Charleston, South Carolina, after deciding to leave the Union.

1860 Railroads

By 1860 the United States has some 30,600 miles (48,960 km) of railroad, though only 8,500 miles (13,600 km) of this is in the Southern states.

DECEMBER 18, 1860, Washington, D.C.

In an effort to avoid a civil war, Senator John J. Crittenden of Kentucky proposes the Crittenden Compromise. This accepts the boundary between free states and slave states. It says that slavery can continue where it already exists. However, it is defeated. President Lincoln is opposed to slavery. Civil war between North and South now seems likely.

DECEMBER 20, 1860, South Carolina

Because of Lincoln's election as president, South Carolina's rulers sign the Ordinance of Secession in Charleston. This is a document that states South Carolina will leave the Union. South Carolina becomes the first state to leave the Union.

DECEMBER 24, 1860, South Carolina

Governor Wilkinson Pickens issues a proclamation. It declares that South Carolina is a separate, independent, and sovereign state. President Lincoln will not allow this. He will now have to use force to stop Carolina. The outbreak of the Civil War is only a few weeks away.

Key People: John Brown

As a passionate enemy of slavery, John Brown (1800–1859) worked closely with the free black community. He acted as a "conductor" on the Underground Railroad. This was a secret network of safe houses for Southern slaves to use as they escaped to the North. He wanted to lead a slave revolt in the South. He attacked the armory at Harpers Ferry, hoping that this would lead to the revolt. But it failed. He was caught and hanged. He became a martyr in the North.

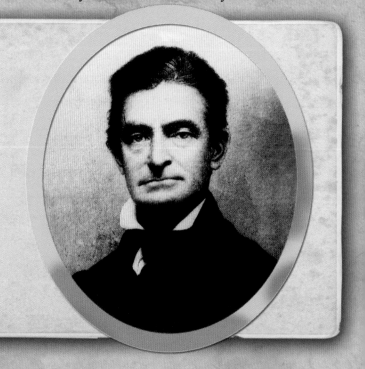

Fugitive – someone, such as a runaway slave, who has escaped from captivity.

EYEWITNESS: Abraham Lincoln, 1861

"I therefore consider that in view of the Constitution and the laws, the Union is unbroken; and to the extent of my ability I shall take care, as the Constitution itself expressly enjoins upon me, that the laws of the Union be faithfully executed in all the States. The Union is much older than the Constitution. It was formed by the Articles of Association in 1774. It was continued by the Declaration of Independence in 1776."

JANUARY 2, 1861, South Carolina
Fort Johnson in Charleston Harbor is seized and occupied by Confederate troops.

JANUARY 5 Alabama
Alabama troops seize forts Morgan and Gaines. This gives the Confederate forces a commanding position over Mobile Bay.

JANUARY 9 Mississippi
The leaders in the capital, Jackson, vote to leave the Union. Mississippi is the second state to join the Confederacy.

JANUARY 10 Florida
Florida leaves the Union.

JANUARY 11 Alabama
Alabama becomes the fourth state to leave the Union.

JANUARY 19 Georgia
The state of Georgia votes to leave the Union.

JANUARY 26 Louisiana
Louisiana becomes the sixth state to leave the Union.

FEBRUARY 4 Alabama
Leaders from the South meet in Montgomery, the Alabama state capital. They write a constitution for the Confederate States of America. Jefferson Davis of Mississippi is chosen as president. He wanted to be a general in the South.

FEBRUARY 7 Alabama/Mississippi
The Choctaw Indian Nation makes an alliance with the Southern states. Other Indian tribes will follow in 1861.

The Union Fort Massachusetts, built to protect the approaches to Washington.

President – the leader of a country.

The Confederates bombarding Fort Sumter in April 1861.

Union troops lie on the ground to escape the smoke. The fort later surrenders. The first shots of the Civil War have been fired.

APRIL 15 The North

President Lincoln calls for the Northern states to raise an army of 75,000 soldiers to fight the South.

APRIL 19 Washington, D.C.

President Abraham Lincoln proclaims a naval blockade of the Southern states of Texas, Louisiana, Florida, Georgia, and South Carolina. On April 27 he extends this to include the states of North Carolina and Virginia.

APRIL 12 South Carolina

Confederates open fire on Fort Sumter in Charleston Harbor. The Union troops in the fort are short of ammunition. They fire only a few rounds from their guns. The Confederate guns start fires inside the fort.

APRIL 13 South Carolina

Confederate guns shell Fort Sumter again. The barracks inside the fort catch fire.

APRIL 19 Baltimore

When Union soldiers change trains in the city, they are attacked by a pro-Confederate mob. Bricks are thrown and shots fired. The mayor, George Brown, vows that no more Union troops will be allowed in the city.

Key People: Abraham Lincoln

Abraham Lincoln (1809–1865) was born in a one-room log cabin in Hardin County, Kentucky. Despite his lack of schooling, Lincoln educated himself to a high level. By the 1840s he was a successful lawyer and congressman. He was elected president in 1860 and was prepared to fight to hold the United States together. Lincoln was a great war leader and led the North to victory. He was murdered in April 1865 by John Wilkes Booth.

Blockade – to use ships to cut off trade or supplies from the sea.

APRIL 23 Virginia

Major General Robert E. Lee becomes commander of land and naval forces in the state of Virginia.

MAY 9 Britain

Britain, wishing to avoid being at war, says that it is neutral as the Civil War unfolds.

MAY 20 North Carolina

North Carolina becomes the last state to leave the Union. There is a 100-gun salute in Raleigh, the capital.

Wisconsin soldiers in the Union army at the Battle of Hoke's Run on July 2, 1861.

JUNE 10 Virginia

The Battle of Big Bethel. 1,200 Confederates beat 3,500 Union troops at Big Bethel Church. The is one of the first battles of Civil War.

JUNE 10 Virginia

The leaders of West Virginia are opposed to Virginia's decision to leave the Union. They break away from the Confederacy. West Virginia is admitted to the Union as a separate state.

JULY 2 Wisconsin

The Battle of Hoke's Run. In one of the first battles of the war in Wisconsin, Union forces push back the Confederates. The battle was fought near Hainesville.

JULY 6 Cuba

The Confederate raiding ship CSS *Sumter* releases seven captured Union vessels in Cuban waters. The *Sumter* is armed with five cannons. She has a top speed of 10 knots and a crew of 18.

EYEWITNESS: Stephen Lee, Fort Sumter, 1861

"FORT SUMTER, S.C., April 12, 1861, 3:20 A.M. By authority of Brigadier-General Beauregard, commanding the Provisional Forces of the Confederate States, we have the honor to notify you that he will open the fire of his batteries on Fort Sumter in one hour from this time. We have the honor to be very respectfully, Your obedient servants, JAMES CHESNUT JR., Aide-de-camp. STEPHEN D. LEE, Captain C. S. Army, Aide-de-camp."

CSS – Confederate States Ship.

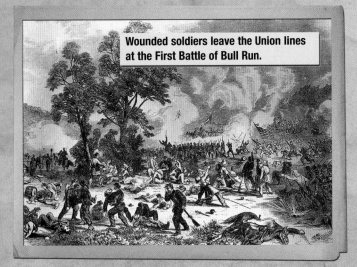

Wounded soldiers leave the Union lines at the First Battle of Bull Run.

JULY 21 Virginia

The Battle of First Manassas / First Bull Run. The first big battle of the war. General Irvin McDowell is the commander of the main Union force of 35,000. He fights the Confederate army of 20,000, led by Pierre G.T. Beauregard. The Confederates win the battle after stopping the determined Union attack. By the evening Union troops are in full retreat toward Washington.

AUGUST 10 Missouri

The Battle of Wilson's Creek. This is the first major battle west of the Mississippi River. It is a bloody affair, with more than 2,500 dead, injured, or missing—among them General Nathaniel Lyon, the Union commander. Lyon is the first Union general to die in combat in the war. The Confederates win the battle.

SEPTEMBER 12–15 West Virginia

The Battle of Cheat Mountain Summit. General Robert E. Lee, future hero of the Confederacy, is defeated despite the Confederates being stronger than the Union side. Union losses are 80 men. Confederate losses are 90 men.

SEPTEMBER 19 Kentucky

The Battle of Barbourville. Some 800 Confederates raid the Union guerrilla training base at Camp Andrew Johnson in Barbourville. But the camp is largely empty.

TURNING POINTS: Union blockade

At the beginning of the Civil War the Union began to block the 187 ports and inlets of the South. This would stop supplies and arms reaching the South by sea. The Union eventually had 600 warships to do this. In the war 300 Confederate vessels attempted to get through the blockade. In 1861 nine out of ten vessels got through. By 1865 only five out of every ten vessels got through.

Union sailors watch out for Southern blockade runners.

Guerrilla – a soldier who does not wear a uniform.

EYEWITNESS: Samuel J. English, First Bull Run, 1861

"On our arrival into the open field I saw I should judge three or four thousand rebels retreating to a dense wood, firing as they retreated, while from another part of the woods a perfect hail storm of bullets, round shot, and shell was poured upon us, tearing through our ranks and scattering death and confusion everywhere; but with a yell and a roar we charged upon them driving them again into the woods with fearful loss."

OCTOBER 21 Kentucky
The Battle of Camp Wildcat. A force of 7,000 Union troops defeats Confederate troops in an action around the Union's Camp Wildcat on Wildcat Mountain.

OCTOBER 21 Missouri
The Battle of Fredericktown. Missouri Guard troops under Brigadier General M. Jeff Thompson attempt to push Union troops out of Fredericktown. They are pushed back. The Union now has control over southeastern Missouri.

OCTOBER 21 Virginia
The Battle of Ball's Bluff. Union forces try to cross the Potomac River at Harrison's Island. They want to capture Leesburg. The attack is badly planned. More than 900 Union soldiers are killed.

NOVEMBER 7 Missouri
The Battle of Belmont. A Union force under Brigadier General Ulysses S. Grant, future commander in chief, defeats Confederate forces at Belmont near the Mississippi River. General Grant is forced to withdraw after a determined Confederate counterattack.

NOVEMBER 8 Kentucky
The Battle of Ivy Mountain. A large Union force fights a fierce battle after being ambushed around Ivy Mountain, Floyd County. The Union soldiers recover and push the Confederates back into Virginia. This battle is also called Ivy Creek.

The Battle of Wilson's Creek marked the start of the war in Missouri.

Counterattack – to attack the enemy after it has attacked you.

NOVEMBER 8 Cuba

The British steamer *Trent* is stopped at sea near Havana, Cuba, by the Union warship *San Jacinto*. Onboard the *Trent* are two Confederate officials, James M. Mason of Virginia and John Slidell of Louisiana. They are going to Europe to represent the Confederacy. They are seized by the crew of the Union ship. The British are outraged because the action is against international law. War with Britain seems likely. To calm the situation the Union accepts that the Union ship had acted without authority.

A volunteer refreshment saloon for Union troops in Philadelphia, Pennsylvania.

NOVEMBER 19 Oklahoma

The Battle of Round Mountain. Unionist Creek and Seminole Indians under Chief Opothleyahola are defeated when their camp is attacked by Confederate troops.

DECEMBER 9 Oklahoma

The Battle of Chusto-Talasah. Retreating Creek/Seminole Indians under Chief Opothleyahola are driven out of defensive positions on the Horseshoe Bend of Bird Creek by 1,300 Confederate soldiers.

DECEMBER 20 Virginia

The Battle of Dranesville. Union troops inflict a sharp local defeat on Confederate cavalry under "Jeb" Stuart around Dranesville in northern Virginia.

KEY PEOPLE: Jefferson Davis

Davis was a well-known national figure. Had the Southern states not left the Union, he just might have become president of the United States. Davis owned a cotton plantation in Mississippi. When the Civil War broke out he wished to lead the Confederate army, but was selected as Southern president instead. After the war he was imprisoned by the Union for a short time. After he was released he wrote his memoirs. He died in 1889.

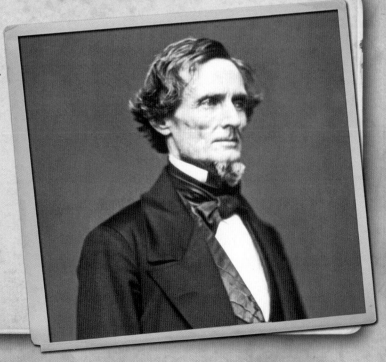

Unconditional surrender – total surrender.

EYEWITNESS: Ulysses S. Grant, Fort Donelson, 1862

"The men who were not serving the guns were perfectly covered from fire on taking position a little back from the crest. The greatest suffering was from want of shelter. It was midwinter and during the siege we had rain and snow, thawing and freezing alternately. It would not do to allow camp-fires. In the march over from Fort Henry numbers of the men had thrown away their blankets and overcoats. There was therefore much suffering."

FEBRUARY 6, 1862, Tennessee
General Ulysses S. Grant captures the Confederate Fort Henry. He has 17,000 men, supported by ironclad gunboats under Andrew H. Foote. The Tennessee River is now a Union highway as far south as the state of Alabama.

FEBRUARY 16 Tennessee
Union troops under General Grant capture Fort Donelson. The fort's commander sends a message to Grant asking for terms of surrender. Grant replies, "No terms except unconditional and immediate surrender can be accepted." About 15,000 Southerners surrender.

FEBRUARY 25 Tennessee
Having lost the protective forts Donelson and Henry, Nashville becomes the first Confederate state capital to fall to Union forces.

MARCH 6–8 Arkansas
The Battle of Pea Ridge. This is the biggest battle to take place on Arkansas soil. Conditions are difficult. The air is cold and much of the fighting takes place in a hollow. Thick clouds of smoke hang low. This makes it hard to see. The Confederates are defeated, losing 4,600 men.

MARCH 8 Virginia
The Battle of Hampton Roads. The Confederate ironclad CSS *Virginia* attacks ships in Hampton Roads. In two hours she sinks two wooden Union ships. The *Virginia* also damages another wooden ship.

Union gunboats bombard Fort Henry from the Tennessee River.

Ironclad – a ship protected by iron armor.

The Confederate ironclad CSS *Virginia* (right) and the Union ironclad USS *Monitor* fire at each other during the Battle of Hampton Roads.

MARCH 9 Virginia

The Battle of Hampton Roads. The *Virginia* returns to Hampton Roads to continue the battle. To the crew's great surprise, it is met by an enemy ironclad, the USS *Monitor*. The two vessels pound each other for almost four hours at close range. Eventually they fight to a standstill. The battle showed that the mainly wooden and sail-powered U.S. fleet is out of date.

MARCH 17 Virginia

General McClellan begins shipping the Union Army of the Potomac and its supplies to Fort Monroe, at the tip of the Virginia "Peninsular." This begins the Peninsular Campaign. The aim is to capture Richmond, the Confederate capital.

APRIL 6 Tennessee

The Battle of Shiloh. General Ulysses S. Grant with his army of 30,000 is attacked by General Albert S. Johnston's 45,000 Confederates. The fighting is heaviest in and around a peach orchard. It lasts for nearly five hours. The buzzing noise of bullets gives the location the name "the Hornet's Nest." The Union line comes close to collapse. But the Confederates are exhausted and halt for the night.

APRIL 7 Tennessee

The Battle of Shiloh. Grant attacks. The Confederates lose all the ground they had

KEY UNITS: Army of Northern Virginia

When Robert E. Lee took command of the Confederacy's eastern army in June 1862, he renamed it the Army of Northern Virginia. In 1862 and 1863 this army won a series of battles. These included Fredericksburg and Chancellorsville. In July 1863 the army was beaten at the Battle of Gettysburg. It continued to fight against greater numbers for another two years. The Army of Northern Virginia was finally forced to surrender in April 1865.

At right are soldiers from Lee's army on parade.

USS – United States Ship.

EYEWITNESS: Captain D.P. Conyngham, Virginia, 1862

"I had a Sergeant Driscoll, a brave man, and one of the best shots in the Brigade. We were ordered to charge, and I left him there; but, as we were closing in on the enemy, he rushed up, with his coat off, and, clutching his musket, charged right up at the enemy, calling on the men to follow. He soon fell, but jumped up again. We knew he was wounded. On he dashed, but he soon rolled over. When we came up he was dead, riddled with bullets."

won the day before and retreat. The South has lost 10,700 dead and wounded soldiers in the battle. They have gained nothing. Union losses are 13,000.

APRIL 12 Georgia
"The Great Locomotive Chase." The Union agent James Ambrose and 22 soldier volunteers steal a Confederate train. They want to destroy sections of the Western & Atlantic Railroad. This results in a railroad chase. The Union men are captured. James Ambrose and seven others are later tried and hanged.

APRIL 29 Louisiana
New Orleans is captured. This Union victory opens up the rest of Louisiana and the Mississippi Valley to invasion. It has damaged Confederate morale.

MAY 31 Virginia
The Battle of Seven Pines. The Confederates fight McClellan's army near Richmond. It is a drawn battle.

Union forces lose 5,050 men. Confederate losses are 6,150. After the battle the Confederates withdraw.

JUNE 12 Virginia
One of the most spectacular cavalry raids takes place. J.E.B. Stuart takes 1,200 Confederates on a daring three-day ride. They scout Union General George B. McClellan's army camped on the Virginia Peninsular outside Richmond. The Confederates capture 165 men. McClellan has been made to look a fool.

A bayonet charge by Union troops at the Battle of Seven Pines in May 1862.

Cavalry – soldiers on horseback.

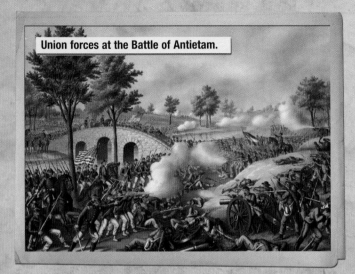

Union forces at the Battle of Antietam.

The proclamation is about freeing the slaves in the Confederacy.

AUGUST 29 Virginia

The Battle of Second Manassas/Second Bull Run. This battle is fought on much of the same ground as the first battle was in July 1861. The second battle lasts two days.

AUGUST 30 Virginia

The Union left flank is crushed by the Confederates at Bull Run. The Union army retreats, thoroughly beaten. At the cost of 9,500 casualties Robert E. Lee has inflicted 14,500 casualties on the enemy. He has ended another Union attempt to capture the city of Richmond.

JUNE 25 Virginia

The Battle of Oak Grove. It is the first of the Seven Days' Battles. That was a one-week Confederate counterattack near Richmond. In the battle General McClellan's Union advance is halted.

SEPTEMBER 17 Maryland

The Battle of Antietam. After invading the North, Lee's Army of Northern Virginia meets the Union Army of the Potomac today. Union forces launch a dawn attack.

JULY 13 Washington, D.C.

President Lincoln reads his first draft of the Emancipation Proclamation to his cabinet.

TURNING POINTS: The Seven Days' Battles

The Union Army of the Potomac was only a few miles outside the Confederate capital, Richmond. General Robert E. Lee seized the initiative and attacked the Union forces. In the next few days Lee's Army of Northern Virginia fought McClellan's army in seven battles. McClellan gave up his attempt to besiege Richmond. The city was safe for the moment. Lee's achievements began to gain European support for the Confederacy.

Union artillery in action near Richmond.

Emancipation – freedom.

EYEWITNESS: David Thompson, Antietam, 1862

"I see again, as I saw it then in a flash, a man just in front of me drop his musket and throw up his hands, stung into vigorous swearing by a bullet behind the ear. Many men fell going up the hill, but it seemed to be all over in a moment, and I found myself passing a hollow where a dozen wounded men lay—among them our sergeant-major who was calling me. He called me to help to carry from the field one of our wounded lieutenants."

At the sunken road the Confederates hold off Union attacks for nearly four hours. The battle ends in a draw. Union losses are 12,400 dead, wounded, or missing. Lee has suffered 10,000 casualties. The sunken road is later called Bloody Lane because of the amount of bloodshed there.

SEPTEMBER 18 Missouri

The Massacre at Palmyra. Ten Confederate prisoners are executed. This is revenge for the abduction and presumed murder of a local Union man.

Lincoln (third from left) reads his Emancipation Proclamation to his cabinet in July 1862.

SEPTEMBER 22 Washington, D.C.

After the Union "victory" at Antietam, Lincoln issues a preliminary Emancipation Proclamation. The final document will take effect on January 1, 1863.

SEPTEMBER 24 Tennessee

Union General William Sherman orders his men to destroy every house in Randolph, Tennessee. This is revenge for Confederate shelling of his steamboats.

NOVEMBER 7 Washington, D.C.

President Abraham Lincoln appoints Ambrose E. Burnside commander of the Union Army of the Potomac. He replaces George B. McClellan. Lincoln did not think that McClellan was aggressive enough.

DECEMBER 7 Tennessee

The Battle of Hartsville. Union troops guarding the Cumberland River are beaten by a large-scale Confederate attack. This Union defeat allows Confederate troops to enter and attack parts of western Tennessee and Kentucky.

Casualty – a soldier who is killed or wounded.

DECEMBER 13 Virginia

The Battle of Fredericksburg/Marye's Heights. Burnside is eager to prove his forcefulness as the commander of the Army of the Potomac. He wants to capture the city of Richmond. He decides to cross the Rappahannock River at Fredericksburg. Burnside has an army of 120,000 men. Lee's 90,000 Confederates are on a hill. They can fire on almost every inch of ground. The Union soldiers make 14 charges, but not one of them gets close to the enemy. By evening 6,500 Union troops lie dead and dying on the battlefield.

Union troops at Fredericksburg.

DECEMBER 14 Virginia

The Battle of Fredericksburg/Marye's Heights. Burnside orders renewed attacks. He is persuaded by his officers that they would be useless. There are therefore no more attacks. The battle proves to be one of the South's most overwhelming victories. In the North morale dips.

DECEMBER 31 Tennessee

The Battle of Murfreesboro. At the beginning, Confederates force the Union troops to fall back. But the last day of the battle results in victory for the Union soldiers. The Union gained control of Kentucky while increasing their hold on Tennessee. It also boosted morale after Fredericksburg. Lincoln telegraphed his troops a heartfelt "God bless you."

KEY PEOPLE: Robert E. Lee

At the beginning of the Civil War, Lee was offered command of the Union armies. But when his home state, Virginia, left the Union he resigned from the army. He was made a general in the Confederate army. General Lee dealt the Union stinging defeats at Fredericksburg (December 1862) and Chancellorsville (May 1863). He was defeated at Gettysburg in July 1863. He surrendered in April 1865, respected by both sides as a great general.

Freedmen – Southern slaves who were freed by Union armies.

EYEWITNESS: Lincoln's Emancipation Proclamation

"That on the first day of January, in the year of our Lord one thousand eight hundred and sixty-three, all persons held as slaves within any State or designated part of a State, the people whereof shall then be in rebellion against the United States, shall be then, thenceforward, and forever free; the military and naval authority thereof, will recognize and maintain the freedom of such persons."

JANUARY 1, 1863, Washington, D.C.
President Lincoln's Emancipation Proclamation comes into effect today. It declares that slaves in the South are free. This means that the Civil War becomes a war for the freedom of slaves as well as a struggle to save the Union.

JANUARY 20–22 Virginia
The Union Army of the Potomac begins to cross the Rappahannock River. The plan is to attack the army of General Lee. But it begins to rain, turning the land to mud. The "Mud March" ends with Union troops returning to their camps.

MARCH 3 Washington, D.C.
The Union introduces the National Conscription Act. Everyone who is chosen must join the army. The only way to avoid it is to hire a substitute or pay a fee of $300.

APRIL 2 Virginia
There are riots in the Confederacy over the high cost of food. They are called "bread riots."

APRIL 17 Mississippi
Union cavalry commanded by Colonel Grierson raids Mississippi. The cavalry rips up railroad lines as it moves south. The soldiers ride south to the Union city of Baton Rouge in Louisiana.

MAY 2 Virginia
The Battle of Chancellorsville between the Union Army of the Potomac and the Confederate Army of Northern Virginia. The Confederates beat the Union right flank. "Stonewall" Jackson is shot by one of his own men. Jackson later dies.

Freedmen joining the Union following the Emancipation Proclamation.

Raid – a surprise attack behind enemy lines.

The shooting of "Stonewall" Jackson during the Battle of Chancellorsville.

MAY 3 Virginia

The Battle of Chancellorsville. The Confederates open the attack again. The Union commander, General Hooker, is stunned when a Confederate shell explodes near him. Union forces are pushed back by the Confederates.

MAY 4 Virginia

The Battle of Chancellorsville. Union forces are close to defeat. But fresh troops appear and disaster is avoided. It is still a great Confederate victory, though. Union losses are 17,000 casualties. Confederate losses are only 12,800 men.

MAY 14 Mississippi

Union troops capture Jackson, the state capital. This is the fourth state capital to fall to Union troops. Union troops destroy Jackson's railroads and war factories.

MAY 17 Mississippi

The Battle of Big Black River. The Confederates lose 2,000 men at the Big Black River. They have failed to stop the Union advance to Vicksburg.

MAY 18 Mississippi

General Grant's Union armies start the siege of Vicksburg.

TURNING POINTS: Emancipation Proclamation

The issue of slavery was at the heart of the Civil War. At the start of 1863 President Lincoln judged that the time was right to free the slaves in the South. Lincoln did not want to make the proclamation while the North was in a weak position militarily. The Union's victory at the Battle of Antietam in 1862 provided the breakthrough he needed. The Emancipation Proclamation also allowed freed slaves to join the Union army.

Fordable – Very shallow river.

EYEWITNESS: *Richmond Examiner* on the Battle of Brandy Station

"The surprise of this occasion was most complete. The Confederate cavalry was carelessly strewn over the country, with the Rappahannock only between it and the enemy who has already proven his enterprise to our cost. It said that their camp was supposed to be secure because the Rappahannock was not supposed to be fordable at the point where it actually was forded. Do the Yankees know more about this river than our own soldiers?"

JUNE 9 Virginia

The Battle of Brandy Station. Union and Confederate cavalry fight a fierce battle. Thousands of cavalrymen take part in massed charges during the morning. Neither side can gain an immediate advantage. As the afternoon wears on, however, the Confederates gain the upper hand. Union forces withdraw. It is a Confederate victory. Union losses are 866 men. The Confederates have suffered losses of only 485.

JUNE 14 Virginia

The Battle of Winchester. This is another Confederate victory. It allows General Lee's Army of Northern Virginia to begin its second invasion of the North. Lee has 75,000 men.

JUNE 16 Virginia

Robert E. Lee orders the Army of Northern Virginia across the Potomac River to begin its second invasion of the North. The plan is to march through Maryland and into Pennsylvania and win a decisive battle there. The Confederates also hope to capture Washington, D.C. Southern morale is high at this time.

JULY 1 Pennsylvania

The Battle of Gettysburg. This is the biggest battle of the Civil War. It is fought between Lee's Army of Northern Virginia and Union General Meade's Army of the Potomac. The battle begins by accident as the two sides run into each other. The Confederates advance from the north but are stopped as both sides send troops forward quickly. Union forces fall back to the high ground to the south of Gettysburg. By the end of the day there are 75,000 Confederate troops and 90,000 Union soldiers facing each other.

Confederate and Union cavalry fight at Brandy Station.

Private – the lowest rank in an army.

JULY 2 Pennsylvania

The Battle of Gettysburg. The Confederate III Corps advances to the slopes of Cemetery Ridge but is forced to withdraw. The Union line holds. In the late afternoon the Confederates attack Cemetery Hill and Culp's Hill. They make no headway. There is fierce fighting around the Devil's Den and Peach Orchard. The Confederates advance to the base of Little Round Top. But Union reinforcements halt their attack. Fighting will resume tomorrow.

An African-American man is lynched during the New York draft riot of July 1863.

JULY 3 Pennsylvania

The Battle of Gettysburg. 15,000 Confederate soldiers attack Union troops from the front. This attack is later known as Pickett's Charge. It fails, and this marks the effective end of the battle. The two armies leave more than 6,000 dead at Gettysburg. This is the turning point of the Civil War.

JULY 4 Pennsylvania

Lee orders his defeated Confederate army back to Virginia.

JULY 4 Mississippi

Vicksburg surrenders to General Grant's Union forces. This is a disaster for the Confederacy. Vicksburg was the city that linked the two halves of the Confederacy

TURNING POINTS: Pickett's Charge

On July 3, 1863, the third day of the Battle of Gettysburg, Confederate General Robert E. Lee ordered an attack on the center of the Union position along Cemetery Ridge. The attack was led by George E. Pickett, who had 15,000 Confederates. As the Confederates moved forward (shown at right), 80 Union guns opened fire on them. Then Union infantry on the ridge opened fire. The attack had failed. The Confederates lost more than 6,000 men.

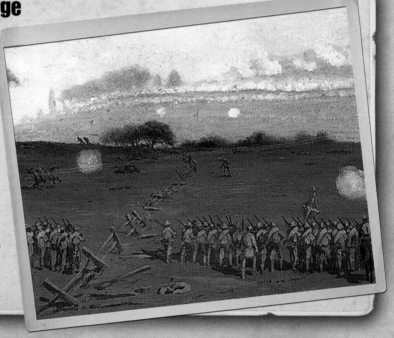

Lynched – hanged.

EYEWITNESS: Tillie Pierce, resident of Gettysburg, 1863

"I had scarcely reached the front door, when, on looking up the street, I scrambled in, slammed shut the door, and hastening to the sitting room, peeped out between the shutters. What a horrible sight! There they were, human beings! Clad almost in rags, covered with dust, riding wildly, pell-mell down the hill toward our home! Shouting, yelling most unearthly, cursing, brandishing their revolvers, and firing right and left."

together. Now that it has fallen the Confederacy has been split in two.

JULY 13 New York

Antidraft riots have erupted across the North. The worst riot takes place in New York. A crowd of angry workers burns the city draft offices. The rioters target New York's African-Americans, who are blamed as a cause of the war. Hundreds of African-Americans flee the city.

JULY 18 South Carolina

The 54th Massachusetts Volunteer Infantry, a black Union regiment, charges the enemy stronghold of Fort Wagner. The assault fails

The Union 54th Massachusetts Volunteer Infantry attacks Fort Wagner.

and the regiment's losses are high. But the regiment's bravery proves the courage of black soldiers to everyone.

AUGUST 20 Kansas

Confederate guerrillas under the command of William Quantrill attack the town of Lawrence. The town is well known for being opposed to slavery. On Quantrill's orders the guerrillas burn the town and murder every adult male they find. More than 150 people are killed and 200 buildings destroyed by the guerrillas.

SEPTEMBER 19–20 Tennessee

The Battle of Chickamauga. In a two-day fight, 65,000 Confederates led by General Braxton Bragg beat 62,000 Union soldiers commanded by General William Rosecrans. Afterward the Union army withdraws into Chattanooga. Chickamauga is a hollow victory for the Confederates. At a cost of more than 18,000 casualties, they can only push the Union forces back to Chattanooga. They do not have the strength to destroy the Union army or lay siege to the town. The Union army has suffered 16,000 killed, wounded, or missing.

Draft – a call to military service made by the government.

Confederate troops attacking in Tennessee.

dedication of the cemetery on the battlefield of Gettysburg. Lincoln praises the "brave men, living and dead," who had fought at Gettysburg. He calls attention to the fact that the living must "be dedicated here to the unfinished work" that the soldiers had begun. He promises "that this nation, under God, shall have a new birth of freedom and that government of the people, by the people, for the people, shall not perish from the earth."

OCTOBER 15 South Carolina

The Confederate submarine *H.L. Hunley* sinks for a second time during a training exercise, killing seven crew members. The *H.L. Hunley* was designed to be hand powered by a crew of nine. Eight men turned the hand-cranked propeller. One man steered and directed the boat.

NOVEMBER 19 Pennsylvania

U.S. President Abraham Lincoln makes his famous "Gettysburg Address" during the

NOVEMBER 23 Tennessee

The Battle of Chattanooga. Union troops push back the Confederates who are besieging Chattanooga.

NOVEMBER 24–25 Tennessee

The Battle of Chattanooga. Union soldiers storm Missionary Ridge and defeat the Confederates. Union forces have secured Chattanooga. The city will be the supply and stores base for General Sherman's 1864 Atlanta Campaign. The South has lost the vital food supplies that were in the city.

KEY PEOPLE: Ulysses Simpson Grant

Ulysses Simpson Grant (1822–1885) was a drunk as a young officer. But he proved to be a great leader in the Civil War. He captured Fort Donelson and Vicksburg and he won the Battle of Chattanooga. In 1864 he was put in charge of all the Union armies. Grant's plan was to grind down the Confederate armies and destroy the South's rich farmlands. His plan worked—the South was beaten in 1865.

Submarine – a boat that can travel underwater.

EYEWITNESS: A.R. Waud, Virginia, 1864

"The Sixth Pennsylvania Cavalry, being in the advance, was fired upon by a rebel force, but drawing their sabers they dashed on, putting the enemy to flight without loss, and the head of the column soon reached the Rapidan. Having captured a wagon loaded with hams and two negroes, the command forded the river without opposition and pushed on, seizing all the horses on their way and all the male citizens, as a precaution against bushwhacking."

APRIL 12, 1864, Tennessee

The Union garrison at Fort Pillow is massacred by Confederate troops. Out of 262 African-American Union troops, only 60 survive. "Remember Fort Pillow" becomes a rallying cry among black troops.

MAY 3 Virginia

The Union Army of the Potomac begins moving south. Grant plans to fight General Lee's army. But first his army has to get through the Wilderness—a marshy area of dense woodland and scrub.

MAY 5–6 Virginia

The Battle of the Wilderness. The armies of Lee and Grant fight in thick undergrowth. During the battle, brush fires become a huge problem. The fighting stops while soldiers of both sides try to save the wounded. Despite this, many soldiers are killed by the flames. The battle is a draw.

MAY 5 North Carolina

The Battle of Albemarle Sound. The CSS *Albemarle* attacks Union blockade ships on the Roanoke River. Neither side wins a victory.

MAY 10 Virginia

The Battle of Chester Station. Union troops fail to destroy Chester Station's railroad.

MAY 11 Virginia

The Battle of Yellow Tavern. A Union cavalry raid leads to the defeat of Confederate cavalry. "Jeb" Stuart, the famous leader of the Army of Northern Virginia's cavalry, is wounded and dies. It is a huge blow for the South.

The gunboat USS *Sassacus* ramming the ironclad CSS *Albemarle* in the Roanoke River.

Garrison – a group of soldiers at a military post.

Fierce fighting during the Battle of Spotsylvania in Virginia.

JUNE 3 Virginia

The Battle of Cold Harbor. The major Union attack begins against Lee's army. It is a disaster from the start. The Union troops are met by a deadly crossfire from Confederate infantry and artillery. Cold Harbor costs the Union army 7,000 casualties for no gain at all. The Confederates only suffer 1,500 casualties.

JUNE 19 Atlantic Ocean

The Southern commerce raider CSS *Alabama*, commanded by Captain Raphael Semmes, is sunk outside Cherbourg, France, by the USS *Kearsage*. The *Kearsage* was hunting the *Alabama*. She finally trapped her at Cherbourg.

JUNE 27 Georgia

The Battle of Kennesaw Mountain. General Sherman and 100,000 Union troops are advancing toward Atlanta. General Johnston and 60,000 Confederate troops try

MAY 12 Virginia

The Battle of Spotsylvania. Grant fights Lee again. He attacks, and there are 24 hours of hand-to-hand combat. This fight at the "Bloody Angle" is among the most terrible of the war. The battle is a draw.

MAY 29 Virginia

By now, the Army of the Potomac is just 11 miles (18 km) northeast of Richmond.

TURNING POINTS: Siege of Petersburg

In June 1864 the Union army began the siege of Petersburg (the siege lines are shown in this picture). The city was a vital Confederate rail center. The stalemate continued until February 1865, when General Grant renewed his attacks. He beat the Confederates at the Battle of Five Forks on April 1, 1865. This threatened to cut off the Confederate line of retreat from the city. On April 2, the Confederates abandoned Petersburg to their enemy.

Infantry – foot soldiers.

EYEWITNESS: *New York Evening Post*, Virginia, 1864

"The Tenth Massachusetts Battery, commanded by Captain J. HENRY SLEEPER, is one of the best in the service. It has been engaged seventeen times since our army crossed the Rapidan, and was one of a very few batteries which managed to get into the fight of Thursday and Friday at the Wilderness. It has come to be called the 'saucy battery' in HANCOCK'S Corps, of which it is part. It is known for its good order and efficiency."

to stop their enemy at Kennesaw Mountain. Union troops attack at a run, using only fixed bayonets. The Union army loses 3,000 killed, wounded, and missing. The Confederates lose only 552 men.

JULY 9 Maryland

The Battle of Monocacy. Confederate troops march up the Shenandoah Valley into Maryland. They want to force the authorities in Washington to move troops away from Grant's army near Richmond. The Confederates defeat Union troops at Monocacy. But Washington has time to prepare its defenses.

JULY 11 Washington, D.C.

The Union defenses are too strong for the Confederates. They are forced to withdraw.

JULY 22 Georgia

The Battle of Atlanta. Confederate General Hood withdraws his main army from Atlanta's outer line. He wants to set a bait for General Sherman to follow. When Hood attacks, his men fail. Hood is forced to stop his attacks. He loses 8,000 men. Union losses are 3,600.

JULY 30 Virginia

The Battle of the Crater/The Mine. Union troops besieging Petersburg set off a large amount of explosives underneath Confederate lines. This makes a large hole, or crater. Then Union soldiers attack. Unit after unit charge into and around the crater, where thousands of soldiers mill around in confusion. The Confederates quickly recover and attack. It is a slaughter. The Union side lose 5,000 men for no result.

The Confederate commerce raider CSS *Alabama*.

Rout – a crushing defeat.

AUGUST 5 Alabama

The Battle of Mobile Bay. Union warships enter Mobile Bay and battle Confederate ships. The ironclad CSS *Tennessee* fights alone against the entire Union fleet. It has to surrender. Union forces have won.

SEPTEMBER 1 Georgia

General Sherman cuts the railroad near Atlanta. He attacks again in the afternoon. This cuts the last supply line to the city. The Confederates are forced to leave Atlanta. They leave that night. Union troops enter the city the next day.

SEPTEMBER 16 Virginia

The "Great Beefsteak Raid." Southerners have been short of cattle to eat. Today, Confederate cavalrymen appear in the rear of the Union army on the James River. They carry off the entire beef supply of 2,486 cattle. The "Great Beefsteak Raid," as it is called, brings relief to the hungry people in the South.

Union General Philip Sheridan in the Shenandoah Valley.

SEPTEMBER 22 Virginia

The Battle of Fisher's Hill. A Union army of 30,000 men defeats 9,500 Confederates in the Shenandoah Valley. Union forces begin to destroy crops in the Shenandoah Valley.

OCTOBER 19 Virginia

The Battle of Cedar Creek. The Confederate Army of the Valley under General Jubal A. Early (21,000 men) surprises the Federal army at Cedar Creek. However, the Union

KEY PEOPLE: William Sherman

William Tecumseh Sherman (1820–1891) was born into a poor family in Ohio. He joined the Union army in 1861. In 1863, he captured Vicksburg and helped to win the Battle of Chattanooga. He was then put in charge of all Union armies in the West. After taking Atlanta in September 1864, he marched to the sea through Georgia. His troops lived off the countryside as they marched. His army also destroyed much of South Carolina.

Regiment – a unit made up of 1,000 to 1,500 soldiers.

EYEWITNESS: General Sherman, Atlanta, 1864

"We have as the result of this quick, and, as I think, well executed movement, 27 guns, over 3,000 prisoners, and have buried over 400 rebel dead, and left as many wounded; they could not be removed. The rebels have lost, besides the important city of Atlanta and stores, at least 500 dead, 2,500 wounded, and 3,000 prisoners, whereas our aggregate loss will not foot 1,500. If that is not success, I don't know what is."

commander, Major General Philip Sheridan, rallies his troops. He launches a counter-attack that defeats the Confederates.

OCTOBER 19 Vermont
The St. Albans Raid. A group of disguised Confederates ride from Canada and capture the town of St. Albans. They rob the bank and then flee back to Canada.

NOVEMBER 8 Washington, D.C.
Abraham Lincoln is reelected President of the United States. He has beaten the Democrat McClellan by nearly 500,000 votes. Lincoln's success is due to Sherman's capture of Atlanta in September. That victory lifted spirits throughout the North and put life back into Lincoln's campaign.

NOVEMBER 25 New York
Confederate spies try to burn down New York. But the fires do not spread. City firefighters put out the blazes wherever they can. One spy, Robert Cobb Kennedy, is captured, tried, and hanged for attempting to burn down the city.

DECEMBER 13 Georgia
Union troops capture Fort McAllister near Savannah. Confederate troops in the city are now surrounded. The Civil War in Georgia is almost over.

A sketch of the "Great Beefsteak Raid."

Sentry – a soldier standing guard.

Union troops camped around Nashville.

DECEMBER 15 Tennessee

The Battle of Nashville. General John Bell Hood and the Confederate Army of Tennessee fight General George H. Thomas and the Union Army of the Cumberland. Neither side can win today.

DECEMBER 15 Tennessee

The Battle of Nashville. Thomas attacks again and the whole Confederate line gives way. The Army of Tennessee is completely beaten. Hood retreats to Mississippi.

DECEMBER 17 Georgia

General Sherman issues a demand to General William J. Hardee, who is the commander of the Confederate garrison of Savannah. The message is: Surrender or face the destruction of Savannah. Hardee refuses to give in.

DECEMBER 20 Georgia

General Sherman orders his troops to completely surround Savannah. He hopes this will force the Confederates to give up without a fight. But Hardee and his men manage to escape from the city.

DECEMBER 21 Georgia

General Sherman and his Union troops enter Savannah unopposed. This brings the Union army's March to the Sea to a triumphant conclusion.

TURNING POINTS:
Sherman's March to the Sea

Following his capture of Atlanta, Union General William T. Sherman planned his next move. He decided to march to Savannah, a port on the Atlantic Coast. This became known as the March to the Sea. On the march his men would live off the land. Between November 15, 1864, and March 25, 1865, Union troops marched 600 miles (960 km) through Georgia and the Carolinas. This showed how weak the South had become. The large-scale destruction, shown in the picture here, also demoralized Southerners.

"Cradle of secession" – name given to South Carolina.

EYEWITNESS: Milford Overley, Columbia, 1865

"During the parley, which, however, was a brief one, we hastily visited different streets in search of straggling Confederate soldiers, but found none, neither did we find any cotton burning. Falling back as the Federals advanced along the street, the detachment passed out toward the east. I remained in the city after the detachment had gone, just keeping out of the enemy's reach by falling back from street to street."

JANUARY 15, 1865, North Carolina
The only major Confederate port still open, Wilmington, is sealed off. The Confederacy has lost its last access to the outside world.

JANUARY 19 South Carolina
Union General William T. Sherman has completed his March to the Sea. He vows to push on through the Carolinas into Virginia. Today, he orders a northward march into South Carolina. The state is considered to be the "cradle of secession" (South Carolina was the first state to leave the Union in 1861). Many Union troops want to make South Carolina pay for being the cause of so much suffering in the country.

FEBRUARY 3 Virginia
A peace conference is held aboard the *River Queen* in Hampton Roads. President Lincoln is attending. Representing the Confederacy are Robert M.T. Hunter, John A. Campbell, and Vice President Stephens. The conference fails to reach a diplomatic ending to the war. The fighting will therefore go on.

FEBRUARY 16 South Carolina
Columbia surrenders to General Sherman's Union troops. The Union troops had fired a few cannons at the city. This was enough to stop the Confederates fighting on.

FEBRUARY 17 South Carolina
As Union troops enter Columbia, someone sets fire to bales of cotton that have been piled in the streets. Within minutes they are in flames. High winds help spread the blaze. Over half the city is destroyed before the flames are brought under control. No one knows who started the fires.

A view of Columbia, South Carolina, after the fire that destroyed large parts of the city.

Skirmish – a minor fight.

Officers of the 4th U.S. Colored Infantry at Fort Slocum in 1865.

resulting from the sudden freeing of tens of thousands of slaves.

MARCH 4 Washington, D.C.

President Abraham Lincoln makes his famous Second Inaugural Address, ending with the words "With malice toward none."

MARCH 13 Richmond

The Confederate Congress passes a law authorizing the use of black troops. In 1864 some Confederate officers had sent a letter to President Davis urging him to recruit slaves. They said: "We assume that every patriot will freely give up the negro slaves rather than become a slave himself."

MARCH 2 Virginia

The Battle of Waynesboro. More than 1,500 Confederates, the last Southern force in the Shenandoah Valley, are captured by Union cavalry at Waynesboro. The Shenandoah Valley is now in Northern hands.

MARCH 3 Washington, D.C.

The U.S. Congress sets up the Freedmen's Bureau. This is to deal with the problems

APRIL 1 Virginia

Colonel Otey of the 11th Virginia Infantry is ordered to recruit and train black units for the Confederate army. It is too little, too late, to save the South. The end of the war is only a month away.

TURNING POINTS: Women spies

Women were some of the most successful spies on both sides in the war. The most effective female Union spy was Elizabeth Van Lew, who operated in Richmond. There were many others, including Pauline Cushman. Cushman was an actress who stayed with the Confederate army and gathered information to send to the Union authorities. Belle Boyd (right) was the most successful Southern spy. She made friends with Union officers so that she could get information from them.

Spy – a person who gets information from the enemy.

EYEWITNESS: General Custer, Five Forks, 1865

"The situation was highly critical, and no one realized the danger more keenly than Lieutenant Blackmar. He had no authority to give orders to advance, nevertheless he assumed the responsibility, he ordered a charge, jumped the ditch and a most brilliant and impetuous charge was thus begun. The charge was made so irresistibly that the Confederates fled in great confusion; the brigade pursued for more than five miles."

APRIL 1 Virginia

The Battle of Five Forks. The actual fighting takes place at a hamlet known as Five Forks, from which five different roads radiate like spokes on a wheel. General Sheridan's Union soldiers crash out of the pine thickets. They break through the Confederate line, killing, wounding, and capturing thousands of soldiers.

APRIL 2 Virginia

Following the Union defeat of Lee's Army of Northern Virginia at Five Forks yesterday, General Grant attacks the Petersburg defenses today. The Confederates begin to retreat from Petersburg and their capital of Richmond today and tomorrow. The Confederate situation is now desperate.

APRIL 2 Alabama

The Battle of Selma. Union cavalry led by James H. Wilson defeat Nathan B. Forrest's defense of the town of Selma. Forrest's defeat is another blow to Southern morale.

APRIL 2–9 Alabama

The siege of Fort Blakely. Fort Blakely on Mobile Bay falls after a siege then a final assault by 16,000 Union troops on April 9. African-American troops play a major part in the final operation to take the fort. There are now 180,000 black soldiers fighting for the Union cause.

APRIL 6 Virginia

The Battle of Sayler's Creek. Lee loses 8,000 men to Union attacks. It is a heavy loss for the Army of Northern Virginia. Many of the Confederate soldiers have no food.

At Five Forks the Confederates were soundly beaten by Union troops.

Impetuous – foolish, daring.

Robert E. Lee signs the document of surrender.

APRIL 7 Virginia

Grant sends a message to Lee asking for his army's surrender. Lee replies that he does not think the Confederate cause is hopeless. But he asks for terms.

APRIL 9 Virginia

General Lee's army is surrounded and outnumbered. He says: "There is nothing left for me but to go and see General Grant, and I had rather die a thousand deaths." Lee then orders white flags of truce raised all along the line. He rides to the small settlement of Appomattox Court House. There he surrenders the first great army of the Confederacy to Ulysses S. Grant.

APRIL 14 Washington, D.C.

President Lincoln and his wife, Mary Todd Lincoln, are watching a performance of a popular British comedy, *Our American Cousin*. The actor and Confederate supporter John Wilkes Booth enters the theater, where he is well known, and makes his way unopposed to the presidential box. Booth shoots the president in the back of the head. He then escapes from the theater.

APRIL 15 Washington, D.C.

President Lincoln, having been taken to a boarding house last night, dies this morning at 07:30 hours. Doctors had tried all night to save his life but failed.

TURNING POINTS: Prisoners

As prisoner numbers rose, both the Union and Confederacy had to resort to using big open-air stockades to hold them. The Union opened Elmira Prison in New York State. It held 10,000 prisoners. By 1864, 1,000 men a day were falling sick in the camp. The Confederates built Andersonville, shown at right, which had 35,000 prisoners. By 1864, 100 men a day were dying there from sickness. Its commander, Henry Wirz, was hanged in 1865.

Stockade – a large prison.

EYEWITNESS: Robert E. Lee, Appomattox, 1865

"After four years of arduous service, marked by unsurpassed courage and fortitude, the Army of Northern Virginia has been compelled to yield to overwhelming numbers and resources. I need not tell the brave survivors of so many hard fought battles, who have remained steadfast to the last, that I have consented to the result from no distrust of them. I earnestly pray that a Merciful God will extend to you His blessing."

APRIL 26 North Carolina

At the Bennett House near Durham, General William T. Sherman meets with Confederate General Joseph E. Johnston, commander of Southern forces in the West. This is their third meeting since April 17. Johnston surrenders. The second major army of the Confederate States of America, 30,000 men, surrenders.

APRIL 27 Tennessee

One of the greatest disasters in U.S. maritime history takes place today. The riverboat *Sultana*, traveling on the Mississippi River north of Memphis, catches fire and sinks. There are 2,000 Union soldiers on board. Most of them are on their way home from battle. More than 1,400 men drown. The *Sultana* was built in 1863 to transport cotton. It was captured by the Union army during the war.

MAY 10 Georgia

Confederate President Jefferson Davis is captured after Union troops launch a surprise raid on his camp near Irwinville, Georgia. In the chaos he grabs a woman's shawl by mistake. This starts a rumor that he tried to flee dressed as a woman. He would be taken into custody and not released until 1867.

MAY 13 Texas

The Battle of Palmito Ranch. Some of the last fighting of the war takes place near Brownsville, Texas. The Confederates under John S. "Rip" Ford defeat a small Union force. There are 30 Union casualties.

The box at Ford's Theatre where President Lincoln was shot.

Truce – a temporary halt in the fighting.

Members of the House of Representatives cheer as the Thirteenth Amendment is passed.

JULY 7 Washington, D.C.

Mary Surratt, Lewis Payne, David Herold, and George Atzerodt, all found guilty of conspiracy in Lincoln's assassination, are hanged at Washington Penitentiary.

NOVEMBER 10 Washington, D.C.

Captain Henry Wirz, the superintendent of the infamous Confederate prison at Andersonville where thousands of Union troops died during the war, is executed for war crimes in Washington Penitentiary.

MAY 29 Washington, D.C.

President Andrew Johnson grants an amnesty and pardon to Confederate soldiers and all those involved in the "rebellion." The Rebels have to take an oath of allegiance to the Constitution. Many types of person are excluded from the pardon. These include murderers and arsonists. Andrew Johnson has taken over from President Lincoln.

DECEMBER 18 Washington, D.C.

The Thirteenth Amendment to the Constitution is passed. This abolishes slavery as a legal institution in the United States of America. Of the 2.5 million men who fought for the Union and 1 million who fought for the Confederacy, 620,000 died in the war. More than 180,000 black men served in the Union army. They thus played an important part in emancipation.

TURNING POINTS: The Grand Review

On May 23, 1865, the Army of the Potomac marched down Pennsylvania Avenue in Washington, D.C. This was called the grand review (shown here). The victorious troops were watched by the new U.S. president, Andrew Johnson, and cheering crowds. General William T. Sherman's Army of the Tennessee paraded down the avenue the following day. Flags were flying from nearly every house as the Union troops marched by.

Amnesty – when people are not prosecuted for crimes they have committed.

EYEWITNESS: Grand Jury report on the Ku Klux Klan

"There has existed since 1866 an organization known as the Ku Klux Klan, or Invisible Empire of the South. The operations of the Klan are executed in the night and are invariably directed against members of the Republican Party. The Klan is inflicting summary vengeance on the colored citizens of these areas by breaking into their houses at the dead of night, dragging them from their beds, and torturing them in the most inhuman manner."

JANUARY, 1866, Tennessee

A group of whites set up the Ku Klux Klan. It is formed by six young Confederate veterans in Pulaski, Tennessee. Soon new members from nearby towns join. They begin to dress in white hoods and ride around at night on horses. They terrorize local black people.

APRIL 9 Washington, D.C.

The Civil Rights Bill is enacted by Congress. President Johnson vetoes (forbids) the bill, but Congress overrides him. The act gives African-Americans the rights and privileges of full citizenship. It declares that all persons born in the United States are now citizens, without regard to race, color, or previous condition. Any persons who deny these rights to former slaves are guilty of a crime and face a fine or even imprisonment.

MAY 1–3 Tennessee

The Memphis race riot. White civilians and police kill 46 African-Americans and destroy 90 houses, schools, and four churches in Memphis. The violence is directed at former slaves.

JULY 30 Louisiana

The New Orleans race riot. Police and former Confederates kill more than 40 black and white Radical Republicans and wound more than 150 at a Republican convention in the city. Federal troops are called, but they arrive too late to stop the killing.

A photograph of Ku Klux Klan members.

Federal – another word for the Union side in the Civil War.

Pupils and teachers outside a Freedmen's Bureau school in South Carolina.

called "Radical Reconstruction." Congress says that Southern states will not be readmitted to the Union until they agree to the Fourteenth Amendment. At first all Southern states refuse to do so.

MARCH 11, 1868, Washington, D.C.

A fourth Reconstruction Act is passed. It proclaims that elections for new state constitutions will be decided by a majority of the votes cast in the contest, not a majority of those registered to vote. The act is designed to encourage black voters.

MARCH–JULY, 1867, Washington, D.C.

The first, second, and third Reconstruction Acts are passed. These acts create five military districts in the Southern states. These do not include Tennessee, which has agreed to the Fourteenth Amendment (see July 9, 1868) and is readmitted to the Union. Former Confederate states give voting rights to all men, not just white men. Also, Confederate leaders lose their rights. This is

JULY 9, 1868, Washington, D.C.

The Fourteenth Amendment to the Constitution is ratified. The amendment grants citizenship to "all persons born or naturalized in the United States." This includes former slaves who have just been freed after the Civil War. South Carolina, North Carolina, Alabama, Arkansas, Florida, and Louisiana each ratify the

KEY PEOPLE: Carpetbaggers

Northerners who went to the South after the Civil War in search of political or personal gain were called "carpetbaggers." Most of these people were motivated by greed. This is shown in the cartoon here. Carpetbaggers served as state governors during the period of Reconstruction (1865–1877). Some carpetbaggers went to the South with a sincere desire to help former slaves. These people were often teachers. Others had fought on the Union side in the war. They also wanted to help former slaves.

Reconstruction – an attempt by the North to make the South more democratic.

EYEWITNESS: Joshua Lawrence Chamberlain, 1889

"In great deeds something abides. On great fields something stays. Forms change and pass; bodies disappear, but spirits linger, to consecrate ground for the vision-place of souls. And reverent men and women from afar, and generations that know us not and that we know not of, heart-drawn to see where and by whom great things were suffered and done for them, shall come to this deathless field (Gettysburg) to ponder and dream."

Fourteenth Amendment. They are therefore readmitted to the Union.

NOVEMBER 3, 1868, Washington, D.C.
Ulysses Simpson Grant, former commander of the Union army, is elected president. Grant will serve two terms that will be marred by scandals. His reputation will later be restored by the publication of his memoirs—among the finest that were ever written about the Civil War.

1869 Tennessee
In Tennessee, an all-white Democratic "Redeemer" government is created. It is sympathetic to the cause of the former Confederacy and against racial equality. Other redeemer governments will be formed in former Confederate states in the coming years. White people in the South are angry about Reconstruction policies.

JANUARY–JULY 1870
The states of Virginia, Mississippi, Texas, and Georgia are readmitted to the Union. They have accepted that black men should have the right to vote.

FEBRUARY 3, 1870, Washington, D.C.
The Fifteenth Amendment is enacted. It gives black males the right to vote. Some Southern states are against this decision. They therefore add "grandfather clauses" to their state constitutions. Typical clauses say that men can only vote if they or their relatives were born in the United States before 1866 or 1867. This is a sly way of stopping black men getting the vote.

Southern women mocking a Union soldier after the Civil War.

Redeemer government – a state government made up of white people only.

A cartoon of 1871 showing the Democrats as supporters of slavery.

APRIL 20, 1871, Washington, D.C.

The Ku Klux Klan Act is passed. It gives the Federal government power to punish people who break civil rights laws.

MAY 22, 1872, Washington, D.C.

Congress passes the Amnesty Act. It removes restrictions placed on Confederate office-holders. They had been excluded from public office by their refusal to agree to the Fourteenth Amendment.

JULY, 1872, Washington, D.C.

The Freedmen's Bureau is closed down. In the South it has built hospitals and provided medical assistance to more than 1 million freed slaves. It has given millions of rations to black people and white people. It has built more than 1,000 schools for black children and helped found colleges and teacher-training institutes for African-Americans. However, it has not been able to protect the civil rights of former slaves.

FEBRUARY 25, 1870, Washington, D.C.

Hiram Rhodes Revels from Mississippi becomes the first African-American member of the Senate.

DECEMBER, 1870, Washington, D.C.

Joseph Hayne Rainey, the first African-American to serve in the House of Representatives, takes his seat. He is a representative from South Carolina.

TURNING POINTS: Legacy of the Civil War

The freeing of nearly four million African-American slaves became the major legacy of the Civil War. The war helped to train a generation of postwar black leaders. In addition, the period also shaped the modern American two-party system. The war brought the Republican Party to long-term power. But it took the Civil Rights movement of the mid-20th century (at right) to continue and finally resolve the political battles begun during the Reconstruction years (1865–1877).

Legacy – something passed on from the past.

EYEWITNESS: Robert E. Lee, postwar

"The duty of its citizens, then, appears to me too plain to admit of doubt. All should unite in honest efforts to obliterate the effects of the war and to restore the blessing of peace. They should remain, if possible, in the country; promote harmony and good feeling, qualify themselves to vote and elect to the State and general legislatures wise and patriotic men, who will devote their abilities to the interests of the country."

1872 Washington, D.C.

Democrats gain control over the House of Representatives and the Senate. This means that the government will not enforce Reconstruction policies in the South. These policies were enforced by Republicans. They were designed to make the former Confederate states more democratic. This meant giving former slaves the vote so they could take part in elections.

MARCH 1, 1875, Washington, D.C.

The Civil Rights Act is passed by Congress. It promises that all persons, regardless of race, color, or previous condition, will be entitled to enter "inns, public conveyances on land or water, theaters, and other places of public amusement."

MARCH 2, 1877, Washington, D.C.

Republican Rutherford B. Hayes becomes president after a very close election. It was so close that the Republicans needed the cooperation of the Democrats. The Democrats have agreed to accept Hayes as presidential candidate in return for the withdrawal of all Federal troops from the South. This is called the Compromise of 1877. This will end Reconstruction in the South.

APRIL 10, 1877, South Carolina

The last Federal troops leave South Carolina as promised. This ends the Federal government's presence in the South. The Reconstruction era is over. Reconstruction has been mostly ineffective. Many Southern states have governments that are not friendly to African-American hopes.

Jefferson Davis, Robert E. Lee, and "Stonewall" Jackson—great heroes of the South.

Rations – the food provided to soldiers or people who need it.

Glossary

abolition ending slavery

assassinate to murder someone by sudden and secret attack

blockade-runner a sailor or ship that ran through the Union blockade of Southern ports during the Civil War

brigade a military unit of around 5,000 soldiers made up of two to six regiments

casualty a soldier who is killed or wounded

carbine a short rifle used by cavalry soldiers riding on horseback

cartridge box a container that holds bullets

commerce raider a Confederate ship that attacked Northern shipping to stop the Union from being able to trade

company a military unit made up of of 50 to 100 men. There were ten companies in a regiment

conscription forcing anyone who is able to fight to join the army. It was used by both the Union and the Confederacy

counterattack to attack the enemy after it has attacked you

division the second largest military unit made up of three or four brigades

emancipation freedom

fugitive someone who has escaped from captivity, such as a runaway slave

garrison a group of soldiers at a military post

infantry foot soldiers

ironclad a ship protected by iron armor

lynched hanged

mine known during the Civil War as "torpedoes,"
mines are explosive devices. They are usually hidden and designed to destroy enemy transportation, such as ships

mortar a type of short-barreled cannon

neutral not taking sides

parole to exchange prisoners with the enemy. The prisoners give their word that they will not fight any more

partisan raiders groups of soldiers on the Confederate side who were told to operate behind enemy lines

private the lowest rank in an army

Reconstruction era period from 1865 to 1877 when the Confederate states were rebuilt and brought back into the Union

refugees people without a home, usually caused by war or famine

regiment a military unit consisting of ten companies of 100 men at full strength. Civil War regiments were hardly ever at full strength

rout a crushing defeat

secessionist a person who supported the secession of the Southern states from the United States and so was a supporter of the Confederacy

segregation to separate people based on their skin color

sentry a soldier standing guard

siege to surround and cut off supplies to an army or town to force surrender

skirmish a minor fight

small arms weapons that are carried and fired by hand

volunteer a civilian who offers to fight when his or her country goes to war

Further resources

BOOKS ABOUT THE CIVIL WAR

Civil War Days: Discover the Past with Exciting Projects, Games, Activities, and Recipes by David C. King and Cheryl Kirk Noll, Jossey-Bass, 1999

Civil War On Sunday by Mary Pope Osborne, Random House Books for Young Readers, 2000

The Civil War (Hands on American History) by Margaret C. Hall, Heinemann, 2006

The Civil War for Kids: A History with 21 Activities by Janis Herbert, Chicago Review Press, 1999

USKids History: Book of the American Civil War by Howard Egger-Bovet, Marlene Smith-Baranzini, and D.J. Simison, Little, Brown Young Readers, 1998

When Johnny Went Marching: Young Americans Fight the Civil War by G. Clifton Wisler, HarperCollins, 2001

USEFUL WEBSITES

www.civilwar.com

www.civil-war.net

www.historyplace.com/civilwar

www.pbs.org/civilwar

www.civilwar.org

www.civilwar.si.edu

Index

A

CSS *Alabama* 31
Antietam, Battle of 20, 21

B

Beauregard, Pierre 14
Boyd, Belle 36
Brown, John 7, 8, 10
Burnside, General Ambrose E. 21, 22

C

Chancellorsville, Battle of 23, 24
Chickamauga, Battle of 27

D

Davis, Jefferson 11, 16, 37, 39

E

Emancipation Proclamation 23, 24

F

First Manassas, Battle of 14
Five Forks, Battle of 37
Fort Sumter 12
Fredericksburg, Battle of 22
Freedmen's Bureau 44

G

Gettysburg, Battle of 25, 26
Grant, General Ulysses S. 5, 15, 17, 18,
    27, 28, 29, 37, 38, 43
"Great Beefsteak Raid" 32
"Great Locomotive Chase" 19

H

Hampton Roads, Battle of 17, 18

J

Jackson, General "Stonewall" 23, 24

K

Kansas-Nebraska Act 7
Ku Klux Klan 41, 44

L

Lee, General Robert E. 8, 13, 14, 20, 22,
    23, 25, 29, 38
Lincoln, Abraham 9, 10, 11, 12, 20, 21,
    33, 35, 39

M

McClellan, General George B. 18, 19, 21
USS *Monitor* 18

R

Reconstruction Acts 42

S

Second Manassas, Battle of 20
Sherman, General William 21, 30,
    32, 34, 35
Shiloh, Battle of 18
slaves 6
Spotsylvania, Battle of 30
CSS *Sumter* 13

V

CSS *Virginia* 17